Who Was
Davy Crockett?

Who Was
Davy Crockett?

by Gail Herman

illustrated by Robert Squier

Penguin Workshop

For the Crocitto-Kenny/Kenny Family—GH

To Mom and Dad. Remember the Alamo!—RS

PENGUIN WORKSHOP
An Imprint of Penguin Random House LLC, New York

Visit us online at www.penguinrandomhouse.com.

Library of Congress Control Number: 2013024953

ISBN 9780448467047

21

Contents

Who Was
Davy Crockett?

Shots ring out. Arrows whiz through the air.
The year is 1813. US soldiers are fighting Creek
Indians in Alabama.

Davy Crockett and a friend stop their horses
across the river from where the battle is taking
place. "Sounds like the major is in trouble," Davy
says. "We'll surround them. Give them the old
Crockett charge."

Davy is a pioneer known for bravery—and
bear hunting. He creeps around one side of the
water. His friend goes around the other way. From
opposite sides, they call out orders.

"Company A! Charge!"

"Company B! Charge!"

Of course, there is no Company A or B. Only

Davy and his friend. Aiming rifles, they pick off the enemy. The Creek Indians retreat, thinking many more US soldiers have arrived. The US major thinks that, too. "You mean there are just two of you?" he asks Davy a few minutes later.

Millions of Americans, most of them kids, saw this battle—on television. It was part of a fictional television show called *Davy Crockett: Indian Fighter* that aired on December 15, 1954. Only four more Davy Crockett episodes were shown. But on those Wednesday nights, at 7:30 p.m., kids across the country tuned in to watch on black-and-white TV sets.

It was just the beginning of the television age, and not every family owned a TV. Still, the

adventures of Davy Crockett became so popular that at one point, forty million people—almost one-fourth of all Americans—watched the show.

The theme song, "The Ballad of Davy Crockett," was number one on the music charts for months. Millions of kids bought Davy Crockett caps, lunch boxes, pajamas, and more.

Davy Crockett was like a superhero. But he was a real person, born on the frontier. He lived in a time when America was still a very young country. It was a time when families headed west to make new and better lives for themselves.

Anything seemed possible.

Davy Crockett became an American legend. Not all the stories about him are true, however.

So who *was* he, really?

Chapter 1
A Pioneer Family

Although he became famous as Davy Crockett, historians say that he liked to be called David. So that's what he'll be called here!

"The Ballad of Davy Crockett" begins with the line, "Born on a mountaintop in Tennessee . . ." Like most stories of his life, it's only partly true. David was born in what is now eastern Tennessee.

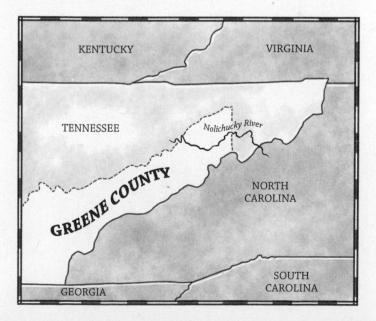

But not on a mountaintop. He was born by the Nolichucky River, in Greene County, on August 17, 1786.

David's grandfather was named David Crockett, too. He came to America with his family around 1725. (The Cocketts had Scottish roots but had been living in Ireland.) In America, the family traveled from Pennsylvania down the coast to the Carolinas. After that, they headed west across the Appalachian Mountains. They were searching for better land to farm.

The Crocketts reached Tennessee in 1776. Today we think of the West as states like Montana, Wyoming, Utah, and Nevada. But in the late 1700s and early 1800s, the West meant land beyond the original thirteen colonies.

Between 1771 and 1772, white settlers from North Carolina began to "squat" on lands in Tennessee that belonged to the Cherokee tribal nation.

Squatters didn't buy land. Even though they had no legal right to do it, they would clear forests, build cabins, and start farms. The squatters also began spreading out to other Cherokee lands, including parts of present-day Kentucky, Georgia, North and South Carolina, and Virginia.

In order to protect their land, the Cherokee, who actually called themselves the Aniyunwiya, fought against the settlers. Many Cherokee towns were destroyed.

In 1777, some Cherokee leaders decided to sign a treaty with the government in order to end the fighting and stop the settlers from taking more land. But then more settlers arrived. By 1790, around 100,000 white settlers had traveled from the original colonies to Tennessee and Kentucky. By 1800, 400,000 white people had settled there.

Some of the Cherokee continued the fight to protect their land. A Cherokee leader named Dragging Canoe led a group of warriors who fought settlers and soldiers until 1794, when another treaty was signed.

John Crockett, David's father, and his wife, Rebecca, lived in Carter's Valley.

Back then, most pioneer families had one-room cabins, with dirt floors and few windows. Parents worked around the clock, feeding and clothing their families.

David was the fifth of John and Rebecca's nine children. Large families were common on the frontier.

The Crocketts were poor. John, like most pioneers, expected his children to work, not sit in a classroom. David had little time for play, and he didn't go to school.

Frontier life was hard, and some years were much worse than others. Sometimes crops did not grow. Then John Crockett would do what his father had always done in hard times: He moved.

Chapter 2
Young David

In 1794, when David was eight years old, John Crockett gave up farming. He moved his family a few miles away to Cove Creek. He and a partner decided to build a gristmill there. The river would power the mill. The mill would grind grain into flour, and the Crocketts would sell the flour to neighbors.

But before the mill was finished, the river rose. The area flooded. The mill buildings floated away.

It was time to move again.

About this time, Tennessee became the sixteenth state. Even more people were traveling through the area, so John opened a tavern along a busy road.

At ten years old, David hunted game to feed guests. He had a sharp eye and a sure shot. Bullets cost money. He learned early to make every bullet count.

Often families hired out children to work so they could bring in money. When David was twelve, he was sent to work on a cattle drive for a man named Jacob

Siler. His job was to help herd cows and bulls from Cove Creek to Virginia, where they would be sold.

David was nervous. Virginia was 225 miles away. He'd be far from his family for the first time. And he would have to get all the way back home on his own.

The trip to Virginia took two weeks. Years later, David wrote about it in a book. David watered and fed the animals and kept them moving. Jacob Siler liked David. The boy was good company, easygoing and cheerful. Siler wanted him to stay on.

David said yes. But he was very homesick.

Weeks passed. Then one day David met some men he knew, who were riding back to Tennessee. Right away, he decided to join them. So he snuck out in the middle of the night. By the time David returned home, three months had passed since he'd last seen his family. He'd seen some of the world. He'd been on his own. Already, David Crockett was growing up.

Chapter 3
On His Own

When David was thirteen, a small school opened near his home. John Crockett let David and his older brothers attend.

The school was only one room. Students learned basic reading, writing, and arithmetic. Some were almost as old as the teacher.

For the first four days, David liked school. He
learned the alphabet. But then he had some trouble
with a bigger, older boy. He decided to surprise
the bully and jumped out from behind some
bushes to fight him. After, David worried about
getting in trouble. Would the schoolmaster tell his
father? John Crockett had a bad temper and might
whip him with a birch stick.

For many days, David set off for school but ended up hiding in the woods. David hunted and explored until school ended. When his brothers walked home, David joined them. He pretended he'd been with them all along.

Finally, the schoolmaster sent a note to David's father. Where was David?

John Crockett was furious. He grabbed a hickory stick to strike his son.

After that, David ran away. He joined another cattle drive. He wasn't nervous, the way he'd felt before; he was older now. He didn't want to put up with his father's beatings. David didn't plan to be gone long. He just wanted his father to cool down.

But after the herd was sold, one job led to another. David crisscrossed states from Tennessee to Virginia to Maryland. Sometimes he helped on cattle drives. Sometimes he took odd jobs.

He liked meeting new people. He liked seeing new places. And people liked him. He was a good storyteller. David was a popular fellow.

Too often, though, David was broke. After two and a half years, he'd had enough. So David headed back home.

Sometimes he traveled on foot, walking up to fifty miles in a day. Once, he nearly drowned crossing a river in a canoe. Finally one night, David saw his family's tavern up ahead.

David was sixteen. He'd grown up. He was stronger and taller. Would his family recognize him?

David slipped into the tavern. He sat down to dinner with the guests. No one took any notice. But then his oldest sister, Betsy, looked at him—hard.

Suddenly, Betsy jumped out of her seat. She hugged David and cried, "Here is my lost brother."

John Crockett was happy to see his son. But he made David work off money that John owed to a neighbor. It took six months, but David paid off every cent doing odd jobs. Then he found out that his father owed money to another man, too. His name was John Canaday. David worked for another six months to pay back that money.

At last David was able to surprise his father with a note. The note said John didn't owe any more money. His father was so grateful, he burst into tears.

David no longer felt like a little boy who had to obey his father. He had done his duty. Now he was a man.

Chapter 4
David in Love

David Crockett did not have much luck with girls. While staying at the Canadays' farm, he met a young girl and fell in love. David was so nervous around her, he barely could talk. Finally he told her how he felt. She listened, but she wasn't interested in David. She liked someone else.

That got David wondering. Maybe girls would like him better if he had an education. So he went back to school.

Six months later, David thought he was schooled enough to find a wife. He knew enough math to figure out money matters. He also had learned to read. Throughout his life, David was a big reader.

At eighteen, he fell in love again. The girl's name was Margaret Elder, and she lived about ten miles away. John Canaday didn't want David partying at night. But David liked to have fun, so he would climb out his bedroom window, slide down a pole

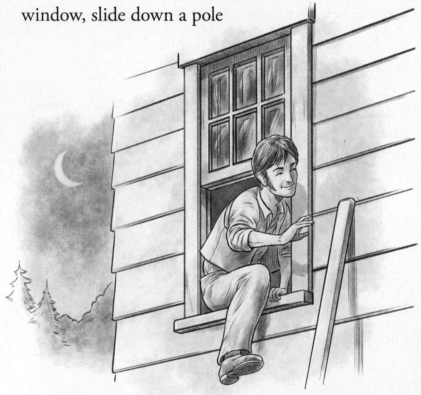

he'd put outside, and ride to Margaret's home.

Margaret seemed to like David. They set a wedding date. Now David had to ask for her parents' permission to wed.

On the way to their house, however, David stopped at a frolic. A frolic was a frontier party where people did work at the same time. It might be a barn-raising, or neighbors might clear land for a new settler. Usually there would be fiddle-playing, dancing, and rifle-shooting contests, too.

David enjoyed these contests and became known as a sure shot. At this frolic, he won a side of beef, which he sold for five dollars. Then he set off again to see Margaret.

On the way, he saw Margaret's sister, and she told him something awful. Margaret had decided to marry someone else—the very next day!

David was shocked. Maybe he should have spoken to her parents right away and not stayed so long at the frolic!

Twice David had fallen in love, and twice his heart had been broken.

But then David went to another frolic. There, he met Mary Finley. Everyone called her Polly. He

asked her to dance a reel. David wrote in his autobiography that he was "well pleased with her from the word *go*."

REELS AND SQUARE DANCES

FROM EARLY COLONIAL TIMES ON, AMERICANS GATHERED ON SATURDAY NIGHTS TO DANCE. IN SQUARE DANCES, FOUR COUPLES FORM A SQUARE. IN REELS, DANCERS STAND IN TWO LINES, WITH PARTNERS FACING EACH OTHER. IN BOTH, CALLERS "CUE" THE DANCERS, CALLING OUT THE NEXT MOVE.

"ALLEMANDE LEFT" MEANS TAKE YOUR PARTNER'S LEFT HAND WITH YOUR LEFT HAND, TURN TO THE LEFT, THEN LET GO.

"DO-SI-DO" MEANS CROSS YOUR ARMS, THEN WALK AROUND YOUR PARTNER BACK TO BACK.

TODAY, MILLIONS OF PEOPLE SQUARE-DANCE AROUND THE WORLD.

After the frolic, David started paying visits to Polly. They talked and talked. Another man hoped Polly would marry him. Polly liked David better, though. They set a date to marry: August 1806.

David had already asked Polly's parents for their daughter's hand in marriage. But it was also a custom to send an empty jug to the girl's house. If Polly's father filled the jug, it meant he approved of the marriage. And Polly's father did!

After they were married, David and Polly rented a small farm close to Polly's parents. They kept cows and tended crops. Soon they had two sons, John Wesley and William. Their home was little more than a shack. Made from pine logs stuck together with mud, it had two small rooms and no windows.

David hunted for food, and Polly made their clothes. But they could barely pay the rent. For six years, they struggled.

Towns in eastern Tennessee, like Knoxville, were growing. But David, twenty-five now, was more interested in the land in western Tennessee. Would it be better? Would there be more game?

The Cherokee were forced to give more of their land to the state of Tennessee. And the government was opening up this land to settlers.

David paid fees and taxes on five acres of state land in Lincoln County. Paying that money meant that he and his family could live on it. In the fall of 1811, the Crocketts moved there, about 150 miles west of Knoxville.

The land was good for farming and hunting. "It was here that I began to distinguish myself as a hunter, and to lay the foundation for all my future greatness," David wrote in his autobiography.

THE TRIBAL NATIONS OF TENNESSEE

NATIVE AMERICAN TRIBAL NATIONS LIVED IN TENNESSEE FOR THOUSANDS OF YEARS BEFORE WHITE SETTLERS ARRIVED. HISTORIANS SAY THAT IN THE 1600S, MORE THAN EIGHTY NATIVE AMERICAN VILLAGES WERE LOCATED IN WHAT BECAME THE STATE OF TENNESSEE. THE CHICKASAW AND SHAWNEE LIVED BY PRESENT-DAY NASHVILLE; THE CREEK NEAR CHATTANOOGA. THE CHEROKEE, THE LARGEST NATION, LIVED IN EAST TENNESSEE. *TENNESSEE* COMES FROM THE CHEROKEE TOWN NAME, TANASI.

David was not nearly as interested in farming as he was in hunting. He became skilled at tracking bears. He learned how to "read" bear tracks, droppings, and claw marks on trees. For the Crocketts, bears provided meat, oil, fur rugs, and clothes. In the land out West, there weren't stores or butchers. David and other pioneers hunted bears to survive.

Still, the Crockett family struggled. Now David and Polly had a third child—a baby girl, also named Polly. When he couldn't keep paying for it, David lost the property. So the family moved to Bean's Creek, just a few miles away. David was still on the move.

Chapter 5
The Creek War

Around this time, a war broke out between the United States and England: the War of 1812, also called the Second War of American Independence.

English ships were seizing American ships and their crews in the Atlantic Ocean. The United States said this had to stop.

Many Native American tribal nations sided with the British. Why?

The British agreed with Native Americans that it was wrong for settlers to keep moving west into areas where the tribal nations always had lived.

There was a war going on within the Creek tribal nation in Alabama. One group, called the Red Sticks, wanted to fight against the settlers and stop the spread of American ways of living. But the other group, called the Lower Creek, had begun to live like the American settlers, establishing schools, creating large farms called plantations, and herding cattle. They liked this new way of life. The Cherokee and some American settlers decided to join the Lower Creek in their fight against the Red Sticks. David decided to join as well. "I instantly felt like

going, and I had none of the dread of dying that
I expected to feel," he wrote later.

Polly cried and begged for David to stay
home. They had young children. She was alone
in a new place with no family or friends. But
David believed it was his duty to fight. So he
chopped firewood for his family and brought in
food and supplies. Then he left.

On September 24, 1813, he signed up with the
Tennessee Volunteer Mounted Riflemen.

The regular US army was busy fighting the British. But volunteers—in groups called militias—fought the Red Sticks. Each tour of duty lasted three months, so there wasn't much time to train. Afterward the volunteers went back to their farms and stores.

General Andrew Jackson was in charge of all the Tennessee volunteers. This was when he and David first met.

David was made a scout. His job: to find out where the Creek were heading. But he became upset. His report "wasn't believed," David wrote. "Because I was no officer; I was no great man, but just a poor soldier." A rich man got more respect; that was "one of the hateful ways of the world."

Among the volunteers, however, David was very popular. He was someone they could count on. One man's account called David "the merriest of the merry, keeping the camp alive" with his jokes and stories. During the harsh winter,

David spent his own money to buy blankets for the soldiers. And he'd go hunting so the troops had enough food.

In November, David was among nine hundred men who surrounded a small Red Sticks town. It was destroyed, a tragic loss for the group.

ANDREW JACKSON
(MARCH 15, 1767–JUNE 8, 1845)

ANDREW JACKSON BECAME THE SEVENTH US PRESIDENT, SERVING FROM 1829 TO 1837. HE WAS THE FIRST PRESIDENT FROM A POOR FRONTIER BACKGROUND. BORN IN THE CAROLINA BACKWOODS, JACKSON WAS A TEACHER AND LAWYER. HE BECAME FAMOUS, HOWEVER, AS A SOLDIER. A GENERAL IN THE WAR OF 1812, JACKSON'S NICKNAME WAS "OLD HICKORY" BECAUSE IN BATTLES HE WAS AS TOUGH AND HARD AS A PIECE OF HICKORY WOOD. IN TIME, JACKSON BECAME A WEALTHY LANDOWNER AND ENSLAVER. BUT PEOPLE STILL SAW HIM AS "THE CHAMPION OF THE COMMON MAN."

David did not enjoy warfare. When the fighting wound down, and a US victory was in sight, he was happy to go home. "Though I was only a rough sort of backwoodsman," he wrote, his family "seemed mighty glad to see me."

His days as a soldier were over.

Chapter 6
An End and a Beginning

David wrote that after the war, "I met with the hardest trial which ever falls to the lot of man." His beloved wife Polly fell sick. Two weeks later, she died. She was only twenty-six.

No one knows for sure how Polly died. In 1815 Tennessee, doctors were few and far between. And even doctors did not know how to treat many illnesses. Smallpox, typhoid fever, and other deadly diseases swept through the frontier.

Heartbroken, David still had to care for his three young children. He didn't want to send them to different homes, which often happened back then. David realized that he needed a new wife in order to keep his family together.

Not far away, Elizabeth Patton lived with her young children, George and Margaret Ann. Her husband had died in the Creek War. She was a practical woman and a hard worker. David and Elizabeth married in the summer of 1816.

He and Elizabeth planned to sell both their homes to pay off debts. Then they would settle farther out west. There was a lot of land to be had after the Red Sticks were defeated.

Once again, David was on the move. That fall, he explored the area farther west in Lawrence County. Thirty-one years old, with a wife and family, he couldn't stay home for long. He'd get too restless. "Itchy footed," a friend would later call him.

David found exactly the kind of spot he was looking for: land by Shoal Creek in Lawrence County, Tennessee.

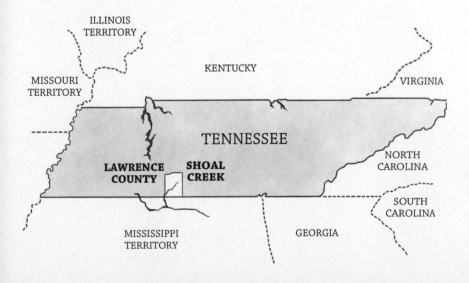

By now David could read and write better than most westerners. He was known to be honest. People liked him. He was good at telling stories. And out west, people loved storytelling. Back then, counties elected colonels and majors to head state regiments. David decided to run for colonel.

David explained to voters that he was just like they were: a simple man. A common westerner. In March of 1818, David won the election. The title of colonel would stay with him the rest of his life, and so would a love of campaigning.

Chapter 7
Crockett Speaks Up

Over time, David held other government offices. It seemed only natural that he would run for the state assembly. Whereas members of the US Congress pass laws for the whole country, people in state governments pass laws that affect just their states.

David began to campaign. Most politicians liked to talk for a long time. Not David. He liked to tell "some laughable story, and quit."

People were taken with David. In February 1821, he won the election. Even so, being a Tennessee assemblyman was a part-time job. He still needed to earn more money.

With $3,000 of his own money, David—like his father—built mills along a river. It was a risky move.

Only twelve days after arriving at the state capital of Murfreesboro, David had to go back home. Summer storms and a flash flood had carried away his mills.

David lost everything. He had to sell his home and the land. David had three more children now: a son, Robert Patton, a daughter, Rebecca, and baby Matilda Elizabeth, and all eight children went to live with relatives.

Elizabeth was used to David's long hunting trips. He'd be gone for months. Still, this parting must have been difficult. But David had a job to do. He returned to the capital.

In the state assembly, David supported some rights for African Americans. He voted against a law that would allow the capture and sale of freed Black people. Slavery, the act of owning people, making them work for no pay, and taking away their rights, was common in Tennessee. Even David—a poor man—enslaved a few people over the years.

At work, David wore plain, worn-out clothes. Other assemblymen dressed in fancy shirts and coats, with cotton ruffles at the collars.

Was David as good as they were? He wanted to think so. And he wanted to convince others, too. Maybe humor could help, he thought.

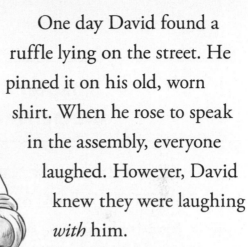

One day David found a ruffle lying on the street. He pinned it on his old, worn shirt. When he rose to speak in the assembly, everyone laughed. However, David knew they were laughing *with* him.

Once a man had called him "the gentleman from the cane." At first David took it as an insult. Cane bamboo grew in a poor part of Tennessee where land was hard to farm. But in time David didn't mind if people called him by that nickname. In fact, he liked it.

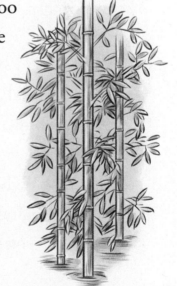

Chapter 8
On the Trail

David had to find a new place for his family to live. In between sessions of the legislature, he rode west with his teenage son John Wesley and a neighbor. They wound up near the Obion River, in northwest frontier Tennessee. It was a vast area of lakes. Its woods teemed with game. David must have thought it was paradise.

Each day David wore a greenish-brown shirt to blend with the trees. He wore soft moccasins to walk quietly through the woods. Leather leggings kept his pants from catching on branches. On one hip, he carried a tomahawk, on the other, a knife. And over his shoulder, he slung a rifle.

David hunted all through the winter. In the spring of 1822, he cleared fields and built a farm. Then he brought his wife and other children.

They had very few belongings. The new home would be plain and simple.

Not long after, David decided he wanted to represent this new region in the state government. His opponent was a rich doctor named William Butler. Again, David used humor and stories to win over people. Soon everyone was talking about the gentleman from the cane.

When the doctor invited David to his house, David couldn't believe the fancy furniture. One rug was so rich and thick! It was so different from the Crocketts' bearskin rugs.

As a joke, David made a show of not stepping on the rug, for fear of leaving footprints. He leaped from chair to bare floor and never touched the rug at all.

Later, David told voters that the doctor "walked on finer materials" than any gowns their wives or daughters could ever afford.

David wanted voters to know *he* didn't own a

fancy rug. He was just like them. Uneducated. A
man of the land, born without money.

David and the doctor were friendly, though.
Together, they traveled from place to place, giving

speeches. One time, David went before Dr. Butler and gave his opponent's speech word for word!

The voters laughed along with David. They also voted for him to take the seat.

David cared about the people in his counties, especially the squatters. He wanted to protect their rights. They'd worked hard and made improvements on the land. He thought they should be able to keep their farms and homes. He wanted to pass a land bill to help them.

About the same time, Andrew Jackson was running for a seat in the US Senate against Colonel John Williams.

David liked Jackson. He was a westerner. Someone who had made his own way, the same as David. Jackson wasn't like the rich men from East Coast cities who had been running the country. Men like John Adams, Thomas Jefferson, and other presidents. In fact, David hoped Jackson would be president one day.

But John Williams already held one of the two Senate seats for Tennessee, and David liked him, too.

"I thought the colonel had honestly discharged his duty, and even the mighty name of Jackson couldn't make me vote against him," David explained in his autobiography.

David was still a Jackson man, he said. But he voted for Williams in this election.

Chapter 9
More Adventures

David had been a state assemblyman now for four years. What would he do next? According to David, he was "called on by a good many to run for Congress."

As a US congressman, he would work in Washington, DC. He could try to get Congress to pass a land bill to help poor squatters in Tennessee.

David had little money to pay for the campaign. Outside David's own counties, the people of Tennessee didn't know him. David campaigned hard. He made speeches all over. He lost, but by only 267 votes. It was a good first try.

In the fall of 1825, David took a break from politics. He had a new idea: he'd make and sell staves. Staves are thin wooden rods that form the sides of barrels. They were made from cypress wood. And cypress trees stood all around David's farm. After the staves were made, he'd float them on boats down the Mississippi River to New Orleans.

David hired some
men. At times, he
worked beside them,
cutting trees for staves,
and helping to build boats.
But "the bears got fat, and
then I turned out to hunting
to lay in a supply of meat,"
David later explained. He
hunted until he had
enough meat for his
family. And then he
hunted some more.
That year, David
claimed to have
killed 105 bears.
Forty-seven of
them, he told
people, in just
one month.

In his book, David remembered one particular hunt he had gone on with a friend:

It was the winter of 1822 or 1823. One night was so cold and wet that David's clothes froze to his skin. Up ahead, David's dogs barked: a signal they'd spotted prey.

David followed the sound. He closed in on a bear up a tree. With the dogs circling below, David fired his rifle. The bear dropped to the ground. But it wasn't dead. It wasn't hurt at all!

David drew his knife, ready for the bear to attack. Instead, the bear climbed down a hole. David jumped in after it. He lunged with his knife. The bear was dead. David's friend couldn't believe the size of the bear. It was well over 600 pounds! The man told David that he wouldn't have jumped in that hole for all the bears in the woods.

When David returned home, the boats were just about built. The staves were ready. And in early 1826, he and his men set off down the Obion River for New Orleans.

At the beginning, all was fine. But then they turned onto the mighty Mississippi River. The boats lost control, pushed this way and that by powerful currents.

David ordered his men to lash the boats together to steady them. But now the men couldn't steer; they couldn't reach land. The boats rushed downstream.

A huge fallen tree stuck out from the water. The boats crashed into it, then broke apart. Both boats were going under. Men were shouting and running around in a panic.

David was belowdecks. He raced for the

hatch. Water gushed through. He was trapped.
In no time, his boat would turn upside down.
How could he escape? David remembered a small
hole in the side, used to dip water from the river.
Could he squeeze through it? He had to try. The
water was up to his shoulders now.

THE MISSISSIPPI RIVER

THE MIGHTY MISSISSIPPI IS 2,350 MILES LONG AND BORDERS OR RUNS THROUGH TEN STATES. IT BEGINS IN MINNESOTA, WHERE IT IS ONLY THREE FEET DEEP AND TWENTY TO THIRTY FEET WIDE. IN ILLINOIS, IT SPREADS OUT TO NEARLY A MILE ACROSS. IN NEW ORLEANS, IT IS 200 FEET DEEP.

THE MISSISSIPPI RIVER WAS NAMED BY THE OJIBWA INDIANS, AND MEANS "GREAT RIVER." IT'S PLAYED A MAJOR ROLE IN AMERICAN HISTORY, AIDING EXPLORATION, TRANSPORTATION, AND SETTLEMENT OF THE WEST.

David stuck his arms through the hole. "Pull my arms off or force me through!" David shouted.

Somehow, they dragged him out, ripping his clothes and skin.

Just as the boat went under, everyone leaped onto a piece of driftwood, as big as a raft. Men from the other boat swam over. All night, they waited for help.

Finally, David and the men were rescued. They were brought to Memphis, Tennessee.

Battered and bruised, David had lost his boats and all the staves. But he was alive, and the people of Memphis welcomed him like a hero. He felt happy and excited about the future. So he decided to run again for Congress.

This time, in 1827, he won.

Chapter 10
David Goes to Washington

David left his family in Tennessee. He moved into a boardinghouse in Washington, DC, where other congressmen also lived.

It was 1827. John Quincy Adams was president. In Congress, David first mostly watched and learned. Bit by bit, he grew more confident. He began to speak up. In 1829, he won another two-year term. He worked hard on the Land Bill, supporting squatter rights.

JOHN QUINCY ADAMS

By now David lived in two worlds. In the world of Washington, DC, he seemed like a plainspoken pioneer. Legend has it, he introduced himself to Congress by saying, "I'm that same David Crockett, half-horse, half-alligator, a little touched with snapping turtle."

In the world of Tennessee, however, he seemed more like a gentleman. He would ride to a frolic in a fine suit. But then he'd take off his jacket, roll up his sleeves, and shuck corn with everyone else.

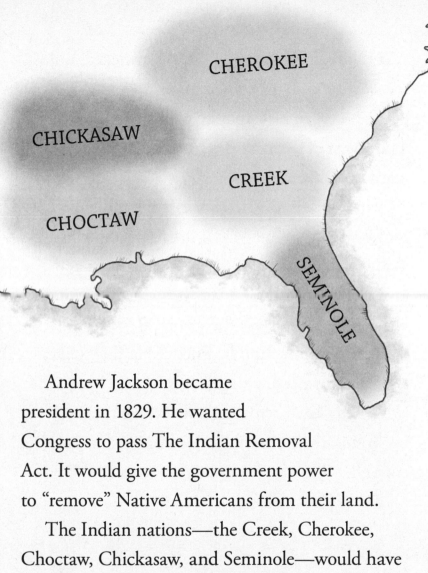

CHEROKEE

CHICKASAW

CREEK

CHOCTAW

SEMINOLE

Andrew Jackson became
president in 1829. He wanted
Congress to pass The Indian Removal
Act. It would give the government power
to "remove" Native Americans from their land.

The Indian nations—the Creek, Cherokee,
Choctaw, Chickasaw, and Seminole—would have
to move west of the Mississippi River.

David said he believed "it was a wicked, unjust measure, and that I should go against it."

As a soldier, he'd fought against the Red Sticks. The voters of Tennessee wanted this bill to pass. It would give them more land.

Even so, David voted against the Indian Removal Act. Why? Was it because he fought alongside the Cherokee and Lower Creeks and saw them as neighbors? Was it because he couldn't bear to see people lose their homes? It had happened to him, and he knew what it was like.

The act passed without his support.

When David returned home to Tennessee, he "found the storm had raised against me, sure enough."

David lost the next election.

TRAIL OF TEARS

THE INDIAN REMOVAL ACT FORCED NATIVE
AMERICANS TO LEAVE THEIR HOMES AND MOVE
TO WHAT IS NOW OKLAHOMA. THE CHEROKEE
NATION'S JOURNEY BECAME KNOWN AS THE TRAIL
OF TEARS. THEIR MARCH BEGAN IN GEORGIA AND
TENNESSEE, AND CONTINUED OVER MOUNTAINS
AND ACROSS RIVERS. FIFTEEN THOUSAND
CHEROKEE TRAVELED 1,200 MILES
IN THE DEAD OF WINTER
AND HEAT OF SUMMER.
THEY FACED DISEASE
AND STARVATION. MORE
THAN 3,000 DIED.

ALL TOGETHER, 60,000
NATIVE AMERICANS WERE
FORCED TO MOVE WEST
OF THE MISSISSIPPI
RIVER BETWEEN
1830 AND
1850.

Chapter 11
Fame, No Fortune

David left Washington, DC, broke again from his campaign. So he did what he'd done before: He sold his property. This time he rented twenty acres by the Obion River. He promised the owner that he'd clear the fields and build a cabin.

Elizabeth and his younger children didn't come. They decided to live with family in another part of Tennessee. David and Elizabeth, though, stayed on good terms. They talked about being together again one day.

Throughout 1832, David farmed a bit, hunted a lot, and kept to himself. Even so, the legend of David Crockett spread. In 1833, a book about him came out. It was a big hit. A popular play toured the country. The main character, called

Colonel Wildfire, was based on David.

David went to see the play in Washington. The audience cheered as he walked in.

When the "Colonel" came onstage, he was wearing buckskin pants and a fur cap. He turned toward David and bowed. David stood and bowed in return.

David was a celebrity. It's no surprise that he ran again for Congress in 1833 and won!

While Congress was in session, David wrote his own book with the help of a congressman from Kentucky. *A Narrative of the Life of David Crockett of the State of Tennessee* was a best seller, too.

Some politicians talked to David about running for president. What a story it would make! From poor pioneer to president! They sent David on a tour of the Northeast. It was his first time on a train. He greeted supporters at every stop.

He went to the theater, fancy dinners, and flag raisings. In Philadelphia, David was given a special gift: a rifle with the words GO AHEAD on its barrel. "Go ahead" was part of David's famous motto: "Be sure you are right, then go ahead." David named most of his rifles after his older sister, Betsy. He liked this rifle so much, he called it Pretty Betsy.

Everywhere David went, crowds gathered. But his bid for president didn't go far. By the time he returned to Congress, David had lost supporters. Some thought he had ignored his job. And David's land bill? After all those years, it hadn't passed.

When the next election came in 1835, David lost.

David was upset and hurt at the loss. "I never expect to offer my name again to the public for any office," he told a reporter.

LAND BILL LEGACY

JOHN WESLEY CROCKETT, DAVID'S OLDEST CHILD, WAS ELECTED TO CONGRESS TWO YEARS AFTER DAVID LEFT OFFICE. HE REPRESENTED THE SAME PART OF TENNESSEE THAT HIS FATHER HAD. HE TOO TRIED TO PASS A BILL HELPING SQUATTERS OWN THEIR LAND. IN 1841, HE SUCCEEDED.

MUCH LATER, PRESIDENT ABRAHAM LINCOLN SIGNED THE HOMESTEAD ACT OF 1862. AFTER LIVING ON PUBLIC LAND FOR FIVE YEARS, SQUATTERS COULD CLAIM UP TO 160 ACRES.

Then he took off for the West to hunt, camp, and think about his future. There, he came up with a plan. Revolution was brewing in Texas. There'd be action. Adventure. A fresh start.

David would go to Texas. If he liked it, he'd send for his family.

On November 1, David put on his coonskin cap and hunting shirt and got his rifle. He mounted his horse. Then, along with a group of other men, he rode off to Texas. He was forty-nine years old.

THE TEXAS REVOLUTION

IN 1835, TEXAS WAS NOT PART OF THE UNITED STATES. IT WAS PART OF MEXICO. MANY AMERICANS MOVED THERE BECAUSE LAND WAS SO CHEAP.

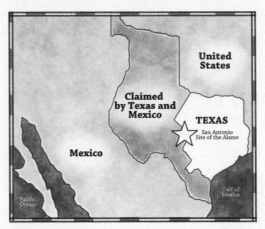

LIKE THE UNITED STATES, MEXICO WAS A NEW COUNTRY. IT HAD RECENTLY WON INDEPENDENCE FROM SPAIN. ONE OF THE HEROES OF MEXICO'S WAR AGAINST SPAIN WAS GENERAL ANTONIO LÓPEZ DE SANTA ANNA. HE WAS ELECTED PRESIDENT. BIT BY BIT, SANTA ANNA SEIZED MORE POWER. HE RAISED TAXES. HE TOOK AWAY FREEDOMS. MANY AMERICAN SETTLERS IN TEXAS WERE FURIOUS. THEY WANTED TEXAS TO BREAK AWAY FROM MEXICO. ON OCTOBER 2, 1835, A NEW WAR BEGAN.

The group passed through Arkansas and crossed into Texas at a town called Lost Prairie. Texas seemed a wonderful place. "The garden spot of the world," David wrote in a letter. Buffalo roamed all over the Texas grasslands. David called the animals "the Texas bear" and enjoyed hunting them.

In Nacogdoches, the oldest town in Texas, he joined an army of settlers who wanted to break free of Mexico. They were heading to San Antonio and the Alamo.

"Do not be uneasy about me," he wrote in a letter to his family. "I am with my friends."

Chapter 12
The Alamo

In 1835, San Antonio, Texas, was a dusty town. About 2,500 people lived there, mostly Mexican families. Just a few months earlier in February, an army of American settlers had driven away Santa Anna's soldiers. Santa Anna was determined to take San Antonio back.

In San Antonio, there was a welcome party for David. At 1:00 a.m. the music was still playing. People danced. Then a scout rode into town with a letter. The Mexican Army was only two hundred miles away. Santa Anna and his army would reach San Antonio in less than two weeks.

"Let us dance tonight," said William Travis, one of the leaders of the settlers. "And tomorrow we will make provisions for our defense."

WILLIAM TRAVIS
(AUGUST 1, 1809–MARCH 6, 1836)

WILLIAM TRAVIS WAS BORN IN SOUTH CAROLINA AND GREW UP IN ALABAMA. TRAVIS WORKED AS A TEACHER, A LAWYER, AND FOR A NEWSPAPER. EVENTUALLY, HE WENT TO TEXAS, LEAVING HIS WIFE AND CHILDREN BEHIND. HE JOINED THE MILITIA THERE, A GROUP OF SETTLERS FROM THE UNITED STATES WHO WANTED INDEPENDENCE FOR TEXAS. BECAUSE OF THE BATTLE AT THE ALAMO, TRAVIS ROSE TO FAME AFTER HIS DEATH. HE'D WRITTEN A LETTER ADDRESSED: "TO THE PEOPLE OF TEXAS AND ALL AMERICANS IN THE WORLD." IT INCLUDED THE LINE, "I SHALL NEVER SURRENDER OR RETREAT." HE DIED AT AGE TWENTY-SIX.

JAMES BOWIE
(APRIL 10, 1796–MARCH 6, 1836)

RAISED IN MISSOURI AND LOUISIANA, JIM BOWIE COULD READ AND WRITE IN ENGLISH, SPANISH, AND FRENCH. HE LIKED TO FIGHT AND GAMBLE AND HAD A QUICK TEMPER. HE WAS ALSO INVOLVED IN ILLEGAL LAND DEALS AND THE TRADING OF ENSLAVED PEOPLE. IN 1827, HE KILLED A SHERIFF WITH A LARGE KNIFE THAT BECAME KNOWN AS A "BOWIE" KNIFE. BOWIE MOVED TO TEXAS, WHERE HIS DEATH AT THE ALAMO MADE HIM A FOLK HERO.

At first, William Travis was in charge at the Alamo. But he wasn't a popular leader, so he agreed to share the command. Some of the volunteers wanted David, but he refused. In the end, Jim Bowie was elected.

Travis and Bowie put a plan in place. The Alamo was an abandoned Spanish mission that stood across the San Antonio River. The Spanish had built missions to bring Christianity to the Native people. Surrounded by strong walls, the Alamo had an old church and a few other buildings. It would serve as a fort.

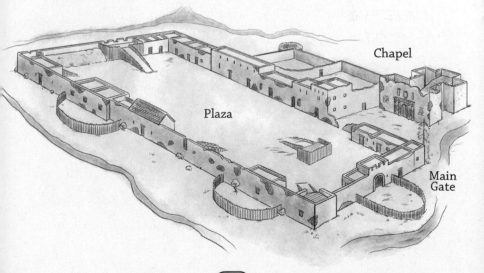

Chapel

Plaza

Main Gate

During the day, the men dug wells at the Alamo. They put in cannons. They made the walls stronger. They worked long hours in the hot sun. David did, too. He helped the time pass, telling stories.

On February 22, everyone in town celebrated George Washington's birthday. They danced American reels and Mexican dances. They ate tamales and enchiladas.

The next morning, most townspeople loaded up carts and headed out of San Antonio. They'd heard Santa Anna's army was just five miles away.

Travis is said to have gathered the men together at the Alamo. He needed five hundred men to defend the fort, but there were only 150. The hope was that more men would arrive to help fight the Mexicans. But that might not happen. Travis drew a line in the dirt with his sword. "I now want every man who is determined to stay here and die with me to come across this line."

David Crockett stepped across the line. So did every other man but one. They were willing to die at the Alamo for the cause of Texas independence.

On February 23, everyone took their posts, including Crockett. Small clashes broke out between the Mexican Army outside and the defenders inside.

After two weeks, not one defender had died. Long days turned into long nights. When the firing stopped, the men fixed weak spots in the walls. Sometimes, David played his fiddle. He entertained soldiers with Tennessee jigs and reels.

But the situation grew worse: Only thirty more men had shown up to help the defenders—not nearly enough. And Jim Bowie had fallen very sick. He couldn't fight. He couldn't even get out of bed. "I think we had better march out and die in the open air," David said at one point. "I don't like to be hemmed up."

On March 6, the sun rose around 7:00 a.m. Shouts of "Viva Santa Anna" and the sound of a bugle call were heard.

During the night, the Mexican Army had circled the Alamo. Twice, soldiers tried to climb the walls. Twice, they were pushed back.

During the third attack, Travis ran to the edge of the parapet. A bullet struck his forehead. He died, clutching his shotgun.

At the north wall, Mexican soldiers put up ladders. A minute later, they were inside the Alamo. When they opened the gates, more Mexican soldiers rushed in. The two sides fought hand-to-hand, with guns and knives. Bowie was killed in his sick room.

Now Travis and Bowie were both dead. Where was David Crockett?

Chapter 13
Folk Hero

Where *was* David? He may have died defending the south wall. Some claim he was swinging his rifle, old Betsy, over his head. Or he may have run from the fort to fight the Mexicans outside the Alamo walls.

One account came from the diary of a Mexican officer. It was translated into English in 1975. Some historians think this report is the most believable.

The officer wrote, "Some seven men had survived, after the fighting ended. Among them was one of great stature . . . the naturalist Davy Crockett, well known in North America for his unusual adventures."

According to the diary, David and the others

were brought to Santa Anna, who gave the order for them to be killed. With swords in hand, a few officers fell upon the defenseless men "just as a tiger leaps upon its prey," the diary went on. Even so, the men "died without complaining."

Is this the true story? No one knows. Only one thing is for sure: David Crockett died at the Alamo.

In April, Texans defeated the Mexican Army at the Battle of San Jacinto. Soldiers ran into battle shouting, "Alamo! Alamo! Travis! Crockett!"

"Remember the Alamo" became a rallying cry for their cause.

Santa Anna was captured. The war ended soon afterward, and Texas became an independent republic. That means it was a separate country. It stayed that way for nine years.

As for the Crockett family, David's son Robert joined the Texas Army after his father's death. Years later, Elizabeth joined him in Texas. The family built a cabin on land Elizabeth had been given for David's service at the Alamo. To mourn David, Elizabeth wore black every day until she died in 1860. By then, Texas was no longer a republic. It became a US state in 1845.

Today, the Alamo is a museum. One of David's buckskin vests hangs in the old church. Cannons

used in battle still stand. It is a symbol of the fight for Texas independence.

SIX FLAGS OVER TEXAS

THEME PARKS AROUND THE UNITED STATES ARE CALLED SIX FLAGS. THE NAME COMES FROM THE

THE SPANISH FLAG: 1519–1685, 1690–1821

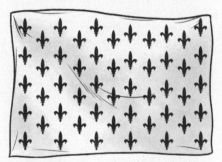

THE FRENCH FLAG: 1685–1690

THE MEXICAN FLAG: 1821–1836

SIX NATIONS THAT GOVERNED TEXAS AT DIFFERENT
TIMES OVER THE LAST FIVE HUNDRED YEARS.

THE LONE STAR FLAG, REPRESENTING
THE REPUBLIC OF TEXAS: 1836–1845

A CONFEDERATE FLAG:
DURING THE CIVIL WAR, 1861–1865

THE AMERICAN FLAG: 1845–1861, 1865–PRESENT

FESS PARKER
1924–2010

IN 1955 AND 1956, EVERYONE
WAS TALKING ABOUT DAVY
CROCKETT AS PORTRAYED
BY ACTOR FESS PARKER.
FESS PARKER WAS FROM
TEXAS AND PROBABLY KNEW
A GOOD DEAL ABOUT DAVY
CROCKETT BEFORE THE
TV SHOW. HE HAD
STUDIED HISTORY IN
COLLEGE. TALL AND
RUGGED, PARKER
PERFORMED HIS OWN
STUNTS ON THE SHOW.
HE BECAME A HERO TO
CHILDREN AND ADULTS ALIKE.
AS MANY AS TWENTY THOUSAND FANS WOULD
GREET HIM AT APPEARANCES. LATER, FESS PARKER
PLAYED ANOTHER FRONTIERSMAN, DANIEL BOONE,
IN A SUCCESSFUL TV SERIES. HE BECAME SO
IDENTIFIED WITH THESE MEN THAT WHEN HE WENT
INTO THE WINE BUSINESS, HIS BOTTLE LABELS
FEATURED COONSKIN CAPS.

The story of the Alamo became legendary as soon as the battle ended. David Crockett had already become famous. After the Alamo, he became a folk hero.

David's autobiography sold like never before. Other books about him were also written. Davy Crockett stories grew wilder and wilder. People said he could "grin down a bear"—make it surrender just by smiling at it.

From 1835 to 1856 there were Davy Crockett Almanacs. Almanacs include calendars and weather forecasts; these ones also told fantastic Davy-tales: Davy takes on hundreds of rattlesnakes. Davy dodges lightning bolts. Davy grabs Halley's Comet by its tail. Davy battles a twelve-foot catfish.

One hundred years later, Davy fever hit again with the TV show.

Over the years, thirteen movies have been made about the Alamo and David Crockett.

David Crockett is both the man of history as well as the man of legend. He is part of the story of the American frontier.

TIMELINE OF DAVID CROCKETT'S LIFE

1786 — Born in Limestone, Tennessee, on August 17

1798 — Works his first cattle drive

1799 — Runs away from home at age thirteen

1806 — Marries Mary "Polly" Finley

1813 — Volunteers as a scout in the Creek War

1815 — His first daughter, Polly, is born
His wife, Polly, dies

1816 — Marries Elizabeth Patton, a widow

1818 — Elected Colonel of Shoal Creek

1821 — Elected to Tennessee State Legislature

1825 — Claims to have killed 105 bears during one hunting season

1827 — Elected to US House of Representatives

1830 — Votes against the Indian Removal Act of 1830

1833 — Matthew St. Clair writes the biography *The Life and Adventures of Colonel David Crockett of West Tennessee*

1834 — Writes his autobiography, *A Narrative of the Life of David Crockett of the State of Tennessee*

1835 — Loses the election for another term in Congress
Leaves for Texas

1836 — Dies defending the Alamo on March 6

TIMELINE OF THE WORLD

Mozart's opera, *The Marriage of Figaro*, is performed for the first time in Vienna, Austria — **1786**

The Irish Rebellion against British rule takes place — **1798**

George Washington dies — **1799**

Alexandre Dumas, author of *The Three Musketeers*, is born — **1802**

President Thomas Jefferson purchases the Louisiana Territory from France — **1803**

Noah Webster publishes the first American dictionary — **1806**

Pride and Prejudice is published by Jane Austen — **1813**

Napoleon Bonaparte, Emperor of France, is defeated at the Battle of Waterloo — **1815**

French doctor René Théophile Hyacinthe Laennec invents the stethoscope — **1816**

Mexico, which includes the land that will become the state of Texas, wins independence from Spain — **1821**

The Erie Canal opens, connecting the Great Lakes to the Atlantic Ocean — **1825**

Former Presidents John Adams and Thomas Jefferson both die on the Fourth of July — **1826**

Wooden matches are invented — **1827**

P.T. Barnum's circus tours the US for the first time — **1835**

The Arc de Triomphe monument in Paris is completed — **1836**

Disneyland releases its first episode of the TV show *Davy Crockett* — **1954**

Theme song "The Ballad of Davy Crockett" reaches #1 on the weekly Billboard charts — **1955**

BIBLIOGRAPHY

Crockett, David. **A Narrative of the Life of David Crockett of the State of Tennessee**. Knoxville, Tennessee: The University of Tennessee Press, 1973.

Davis, William G. **Three Roads to the Alamo: The Lives of David Crockett, James Bowie, and William Barret Travis**. New York: HarperCollins Publishers, 1998.

Shackford, James Atkins. **David Crockett: The Man and the Legend**. Lincoln, Nebraska: University of Nebraska Press, 1986.

*Sullivan, George. **Davy Crockett**. New York: Scholastic Press, 2001.

Wallis, Michael. **David Crockett**. New York: W.W. Norton & Company, 2011.

*Winders, Richard Bruce. **Davy Crockett: The Legend of the Wild Frontier**. New York: The Rosen Publishing Group, 2003.

*The starred books are for young readers.

WHOHQ

YOUR HEADQUARTERS FOR HISTORY

Activities, Mad Libs, and sidesplitting jokes!
Discover the Who HQ books beyond the biographies

Who? What? Where?

Learn more at whohq.com!